Meet the Methodists

An Introduction to The United Methodist Church

Charles L. Allen

ABINGDON PRESS

Nashville

MEET THE METHODISTS

Copyright ©1986 by Abingdon Press

Third Printing 1986

This book is printed on acid-free paper.

Library of Congress Cataloging in Publication Data

Allen, Charles Livingstone, 1913-
    Meet the Methodists.
    1. Methodist Church. 2. United Methodist Church
(U.S.)
I. Title. II. Title: United Methodist primer.
BX8331.2.A44   1986   287'.6   85-28794

ISBN 0-687-24650-4 (pbk.: alk. paper)

Scripture quotations unless otherwise noted are from the Revised Standard
Version of the Bible, copyrighted 1946, 1952, © 1971, 1973 by the Division of
Christian Education of the National Council of the Churches of Christ in the
U.S.A. and are used by permission.

Scripture quotations noted NEB are from the New English Bible. © the
Delegates of the Oxford University Press and the Syndics of the Cambridge
University Press 1961, 1970. Reprinted by permission.

MANUFACTURED BY THE PARTHENON PRESS AT
NASHVILLE, TENNESSEE, UNITED STATES OF AMERICA

In memory of
the Reverend J. R. Allen, my father
and
Bishop Marvin A. Franklin, my uncle

CONTENTS

PREFACE

In writing these pages I was guided by previous *Primers* written by Bishop Charles Claude Selecman, Bishop Paul Washburn, and Bishop James Armstrong. Each of these editions was extremely well written and rendered great service to the Church. From the previous editions I have both quoted and used ideas and thoughts.

From the foreword of *The John Wesley Reader*, compiled by Al Bryant (Word Books), I have used some material which I had earlier written for that volume.

The Book of Discipline of The United Methodist Church is a magnificent publication. I have used it frequently in writing these pages. I urge members of our church to obtain a *Discipline*. Reading it will be interesting, educational, and inspiring.

During this endeavor, I found myself re-reading with renewed interest notes I took in my church history classes at Candler School of Theology. My professor was William T. Watkins—a truly great teacher.

I express appreciation to Mrs. Mildred Parker for her assistance in preparing this manuscript.

In writing these pages, my understanding and appreciation of my church has increased.

Charles L. Allen
5100 San Felipe, #182
Houston, Texas 77056

I

THE CHURCH

The United Methodist Church is part of a tradition which has been an activity of human beings as far back in history as can be traced. As far as we can ascertain, all people who have ever lived on this earth have had some form of worship of God.

In the very creation of human beings, there was put in them an instinctive belief in a higher power. Nowhere in the Bible are we commanded to believe in God; that is taken for granted. People use different names for God, but all instinctively believe. In every society of which history knows, there have been some people who would worship together the higher power in which they believed. That practice has continued to this day.

There are several major religions held by people on the earth today—Buddhism, Hinduism, Islam, Judaism, and Christianity, as well as some others. The United Methodist Church is part of the stream of faith which includes Abraham, Moses, David, and the prophets. We, along with Judaism, hold the Old Testament to be the Word of God. But we believe that a major new beginning on this earth took place in the coming of Jesus Christ, as recorded in the New Testament. "For God so loved the world that he gave his only Son, that whoever believes in him should not perish but have eternal life" (John 3:16).

Jesus Christ is the beginning of the Christian faith. Jesus asked his disciples:

"But who do you say that I am?" Simon Peter replied, "You are the Christ, the Son of the living God." And Jesus answered him, "Blessed are you, Simon Bar-Jona! For flesh and blood has not revealed this to you, but my Father who is in heaven. . . . You are Peter, and on this rock I will build my church, and the powers of death shall not prevail against it." (Matthew 16:15-18)

The United Methodist Church is part of the Christian faith and of the church which Jesus built on the foundation of belief in him, the Son of the living God. The beginnings of the church are recorded in the book of Acts.

In 1517, Martin Luther nailed his ninety-five theses to the door of the church in Wittenburg, Germany, protesting against abuses in the Catholic Church. (Eventually his followers were called Lutherans.) Thus began the part of the Christian faith that is known as the Protestant church. In the same century, John Calvin broke with Catholicism, becoming the father of the Reformed tradition (including Presbyterianism); and King Henry VIII of England took over the headship of the church in his country, forming the Anglican Church (Church of England), known in its branches outside of England as the Episcopal Church. The United Methodist Church is part of the Protestant church and traces its history back to the Anglican Church.

THE FIRST METHODIST SOCIETY

John Wesley, the founder of The Methodist Church, who was himself an Anglican priest, wrote the following account of the first society called Methodist:

"In November, 1729, four young gentlemen of Oxford—
Mr. John Wesley, Fellow of Lincoln College; Mr. Charles
Wesley, Student of Christ Church; Mr. Morgan, Com-
moner of Christ Church; and Mr. Kirkman, of Merton
College—began . . . reading chiefly the Greek Testament. The next year, two or three of Mr. Wesley's pupils
desired the liberty of meeting with them; and afterwards
one of Mr. Charles Wesley's pupils. It was in 1732 that
Mr. Ingham, of Queens's College, and Mr. Broughton, of
Exeter, were added to their number. To these, in April,
was joined Mr. Clayton of Brazen-nose, with two or three
of his pupils. About the same time Mr. James Hervey was
permitted to meet with them, and afterwards Mr.
Whitefield."

This club was started by Charles Wesley during the
second year of his student life at Oxford (1727). He
persuaded two or three others to join with him in
organizing a society. They met first every Sunday
evening, then two evenings a week, and finally every
evening from six until nine o'clock. Their meetings and
deportment attracted the attention of both faculty and
students. One of the students said, "Here is a new sect of
Methodists sprung up."

John Wesley was not at Oxford when the society was
first formed. When he returned, he immediately associated himself with the society and was recognized as its
head. Their activities included the study of the Bible in
Hebrew and Greek; the study of the classics; visits to the
prison and the poor and the sick; and religious instruction
of poor children. At the time the work of the society was so

novel that the news of it spread beyond Oxford. They met with both praise and harsh criticism. The society was called by various names, such as Bible Moths, The Reformers' Club, The Godly Club, The Enthusiasts, and The Holy Club; but the name Methodists stuck. Though it was sometimes applied in derision, the Wesleys welcomed the term. Today millions of people in all parts of the world are happy to bear the name.

(Bishop Charles C. Selecman, *The Methodist Primer*, 1944)

WHY THE CHURCH?

Why is there such an organization as the church? Why does the church continue? Here are some answers to these questions:

(1) There is no such thing as a solitary religion. Religious faith is both love for God and love for people. The church provides for both expressions of love.

(2) The church is necessary to human nature. Human beings have strong urges toward both the self and the group. Persons have a social instinct which is frustrated if they do not work out their spiritual life in corporate fellowship. Private devotions and corporate communion with God are both necessary expressions of human beings.

(3) The church is the extension of the incarnation of God: "And the Word became flesh and dwelt among us" (John 1:14). Just as Christ is the incarnation of God, so the church is the incarnation of Christ—thus we speak of

the church as "the body of Christ." The Christian church is a physical representative of Christ on this earth.

(4) The church is the best serving institution this world has ever known. Education for the masses was begun by the church, as were hospitals, children's homes, and charitable institutions too numerous to mention. Church people are people who care about other people.

(5) The church contains the best human life in the world. There are some exceptions both in and out of the church—but they *are* exceptions. The Christian faith offers people the motive and the power to change and transform their lives.

(6) The church is the one unbroken fellowship in the world. The *Epistle to Diognetus* was written at the time when the military might of the Roman Empire was falling to pieces. In that epistle we read, "What the soul is to the body, so the Christians are to the world—they hold the world together."

The words of Celsus, spoken in the second century, are just as true today, "The Christians love each other even before they are acquainted." Love for God and for one another—they go together.

(7) The church gives a sense of solidarity to all the centuries. The Bible was written for a people many years ago; yet it is no less applicable to the lives of people today. When Paul speaks of "we," he is referring to people of his day; his references, however, include all of us in this day as well. Today when Christians use the term "we," it

includes not only us in the church today, but also our parents, grandparents, and even the first apostles. Likewise our "we" includes our children and even generations yet unborn. The church links all children of God into one unbroken stream. Jesus refers to this when he prays not only for his disciples but for all who would believe through their word (John 17:20).

(8) The denomination is not the church. We Methodists believe we are part of the family of Christians. Christians give allegiance to the church through a denomination.

(9) The church is not the kingdom of God. God brings God's kingdom. Christians pray, "Thy kingdom come." The purpose of the church is to help people enter God's kingdom. As part of God's kingdom, we serve humanity.

Recently I was driving in the country of Jordan. I stopped in a small community for lunch. Before getting back to my car, I saw about twenty school children coming down the street. They were happy, laughing children. Walking over to the children, I began talking with them, but there was an insurmountable language barrier. Then I held out my arms, and four of the little children came to me smiling. There with them I realized those little Moslem children belong to God, too.

(10) We believe in eternal life. The church is the most effective voice on earth that assures us of the fact of eternal life.

THE HOLY CATHOLIC CHURCH

The Apostles' Creed is a confession of faith for many Christian churches. In the Apostles' Creed, United Methodist churches join with many other churches in confessing their faith in "the holy catholic Church." Those words do not refer to the Roman Catholic Church; they mean that beyond our loyalty to our own denomination, we believe in the Church Universal.

II

THE UNITED METHODIST CHURCH

The United Methodist Church began with John Wesley. To understand the church it is necessary to know about him. He was born in Epworth, England, June 17, 1703. He died in London, March 2, 1791. Those eighty-eight years contain a most remarkable life.

His first ten years were spent in the parsonage in Epworth, in Norfolk County, where his father, the Reverend Samuel Wesley, a minister in the Church of England, was rector. Perhaps no experience affected Wesley's life more than the one that occurred on February 9, 1709, when he was not quite six years old. The family home was on fire. It was thought that all the family were safely out of the house. Then it was discovered that John was trapped in an upstairs room. He was rescued, and on the very spot—as the house was burning—his mother dedicated the child to God anew, saying he was "a brand plucked out of the burning."

John Wesley was no self-made man. He attended Charterhouse and Oxford University. Those were two of the finest schools in all the world. There, his acute mind and sensitive soul were greatly influenced by a very thorough formal education. His father, grandfather, and great-grandfather had been Oxford men before him, and he was proud to be in the Oxford tradition. He gained a reputation for scholarship and became an intellectually outstanding man.

During the next nine years he served as a fellow of Lincoln College, with a brief interim as his father's assistant in the capacity of parish clergyman. Later he came to Savannah, Georgia, as a missionary, and here we see the beginning of the breakdown of Wesley's high-church religion. His ministry in Georgia was not successful. He wrote in his journal, "Why (what was least of all expected), that I, who went to America to convert others, was never myself converted to God," though later he wrote in the margin, "I doubt this."

In Savannah, Wesley came to know a Moravian pastor by the name of August Spangenberg. On the ship coming to Georgia, Wesley had found himself cringing with fear in the midst of a storm, but the Moravians on board faced the peril with perfect poise. The fact that they were different from himself broke Wesley's pride. Upon his return to England, he came to know a very outstanding Moravian, Peter Böhler, who had come there from Frankfurt, Germany.

ALDERSGATE

The story here must be told in Wesley's own words:

In the evening I went very unwillingly to a society in Aldersgate Street, where one was reading Luther's preface to the *Epistle to the Romans*. About a quarter before nine, while he was describing the change which God works in the heart through faith in Christ, I felt my heart strangely warmed. I felt I did trust in Christ, Christ

alone for salvation; and an assurance was given me that
He had taken away *my* sins, even *mine*, and saved *me*
from the law of sin and death.

I began to pray with all my might for those who had in a
more especial manner despitefully used me and perse-
cuted me. I then testified openly to all there what I now
first felt in my heart.

This was on Wednesday evening, May 24, 1738. That
was the rising of the sun in John Wesley's life—the sun
that never set.

Today as we look back on the eighteenth century, we
see three great movements: the rise of the Anglo-Saxon
nations (specifically the expansion of the British Empire
and the rise of the United States), the rise of Methodism,
and the rise of the great modern missionary movement.
John Wesley might say of all of them, *Quorem pars
magna fui* (Of which things I was an important part).
These three were believed to converge upon a common
object—the salvation of mankind. Wesley expressed this
view in saying, "The world is my parish," which words he
spoke in front of his father's church at Epworth. Each of
these three movements would have suffered without the
support of the others.

FOUR MOMENTOUS DECISIONS

During the year following his Aldersgate experience,
John Wesley made four momentous decisions, which
eventually led to the founding and worldwide mission of
The Methodist Church:

First, he approved field preaching. He found himself

shut out of the churches because of the content of his preaching, so he took to the open fields. Wesley's high-church scruples against preaching anywhere but in a pulpit were melted away by the opportunities of evangelism. This was the forerunner of revivalism.

Second, he approved of lay preaching. It would have been utterly impossible to get ordained ministers to carry on this new movement. People were being converted and needed biblical teaching. To permit the unordained to preach was scandalous to high-church officials, but John Wesley stood by that decision.

Third, Wesley decided to organize converts and give them some kind of supervision. He became a practical churchman.

Fourth, Wesley decided to house his societies. The actual beginning of the world's first Methodist chapel was at Bristol, May 12, 1739. Later a chapel was built in London—the Foundry—and soon a second chapel was built in London. From such beginnings, the housing of Methodism went on.

Was Wesley conscious of the significance of what he was doing? The answer is no. Like Abraham, the father of the faithful, he rose at the call of God and went out, knowing not whither. Those who are dedicated to God never worry about what the results will be. This brings to mind such notables as Moses at the burning bush, Paul on the road to Damascus, and men like Martin Luther and John Calvin and John Knox. Like them, Wesley became a hero of the faith.

John Wesley never professed to discover new truths; he was concerned to restore the old faith. He was no innovator, but a renovator. As one reads the excellent collection of readings from John Wesley's sermons and journals, two errors concerning John Wesley and Methodism are completely dispelled. Some have thought that Wesley cared nothing for doctrinal truth and that he made Methodism a movement of doctrineless sentiment and creedless enthusiasm. Others have imagined that Wesley preached new doctrines never known to the church before his time, and that Methodism came from this new teaching. Both of these ideas are completely in error. Wesley's preaching and teaching were based on the teaching of Scripture.

DOCTRINES WESLEY PREACHED

Here let us sum up very briefly the doctrines that John Wesley preached:

(1) The doctrine of the authority and inspiration of the Holy Scriptures.

(2) The doctrine of the depravity of human nature and inability of persons to turn to God without the aid of the Holy Spirit.

(3) The doctrine of the atonement of Christ, made through his vicarious sacrifice for the sin of the world, which is the sole meritorious cause for human acceptance with God.

(4) The doctrine of the universality of that atonement, whereby "whoever believes . . . shall not perish but have eternal life."

(5) The doctrine of justification by faith alone as the instrumental cause of a person's salvation.

(6) The doctrine of new birth and the absolute need of a conscious conversion or regeneration.

(7) The doctrine of sanctification by the cleansing power of the Holy Ghost through faith in Christ.

(8) The doctrine of the witness of the Spirit, bearing witness with the spirit of a regenerated person that he or she is a child of God.

John Wesley met the needs of his day and generation, with its masses of people who were defeated. He declared the availability of God's grace for all people—that every person is a child of God. To the churches he proclaimed a salvation that would make religion a power instead of a burden, that would lift religion from drudgery to joyful fellowship with God. The gospel that John Wesley preached was "good news" to the people of his day. His translation of Christ and his message into terms which promised people of his century salvation literally transformed a century.

One thing further—John Wesley was concerned with the society in which he lived. For him religion was not merely an emotional experience; it was a program of action that called for a plan of attack wherever an evil was damaging the lives of people. He especially waged his fight against what he regarded as the four greatest evils of his age: poverty, war, ignorance, and disease. After more than a half century of war against these evils, one can say that the modern social conscience had been born.

Wesley claimed that each person is a "steward" of wealth, not an owner. It has been claimed that Wesley was the founder of modern philanthropy and that his

attitude toward human need was far in advance of the
older attitude of almsgiving charity.

Wesley was an untiring enemy of ignorance. It was his
theory that every person is entitled to the blessing of
education. It may be that his theories of education were
lacking at some points, but his conviction as to who
should be educated gives him a place in the history of
education. Green, the historian, states, "Wesley gave the
first impulse to our popular education."

Wesley was not a pacifist in the modern sense, but he
believed passionately that people of reason ought to be
able to settle their differences. To Wesley's mind, war was
insanity. He felt there was no need to discuss war in
relation to religion. War stood condemned on the basis of
"common sense."

Wesley was deeply concerned with human suffering.
In London he organized a group of volunteers who
systematically visited the sick. London was divided into
twenty-three sections, with two visitors assigned to each
section. They were instructed not only to inquire into the
spiritual state of the sick, but also to discover their trouble
and to seek medical advice, to relieve them if they were in
want, and to render any other needed service. John
Wesley believed in a practical application of Christianity.
(These principles are discussed more fully in chapter 6 of
this book.)

THE WESLEY FAMILY

John Wesley was the son of Samuel Wesley, the
grandson of John Wesley, and the great grandson of

Bartholomew Wesley, all three of whom were graduates of Oxford University and clergymen in the Church of England.

John Wesley's mother was Susanna Annesley Wesley, the daughter of Dr. Samuel Annesley, an English clergyman. She received an excellent education and became a wonderful teacher. She taught each of her many children to read at the age of five, and all were educated at home. She was extremely thorough as a teacher and gave to all her children, including John, a wonderful educational and spiritual background.

John's most famous brother was Charles, who was five years younger. Charles wrote the hymns for the early Methodists—many of which are now in our present United Methodist *Book of Hymns*. Among his best loved hymns are "Jesus, Lover of My Soul," "Love Divine, All Loves Excelling," "A Charge to Keep I Have," "O for a Thousand Tongues to Sing," and "Hark, the Herald Angels Sing." It is said that Charles Wesley wrote 6,500 hymns.

A CHURCH BEGINS

John Wesley did not plan to found a new church. He felt God had called him to preach the gospel of Jesus Christ as an ordained minister in the Church of England, and to minister to those whom he won to the Christian life. To do that, he gathered the new converts in groups, classes, and societies, and appointed lay people as leaders. He encouraged those whom he had chosen to preach to the people on the streets, in homes, wherever there was opportunity. Once a year he called these leaders together for a conference. Only after Wesley's death did the new leaders of Wesley's societies decide to leave the Church of England and become The Methodist Church.

Wesley emphasized three important activities:

(1) *Evangelism*—"The world is my parish," he said over and over. He did not wait for the people to come to him or to the meetings. He preached and practiced going out to find the people.

(2) *Organization and administration*—In this way the fruits of evangelism were conserved and extended.

(3) *Education*—He believed in teaching and learning. The printed page was most important in Wesley's life.

THE UNITED SOCIETY

The opposition by the established church to Wesley's preaching and the persecution of new Christians only intensified the zeal of the Methodists and served to spread the news of their work throughout England.

Naturally the followers of Wesley, having received new faith and hope, would come together to exchange their experiences and talk of their new relation to God. This gave rise to the organization of [Methodist] societies in London, Bristol, and other towns and villages. Methodist chapels were also built. The cornerstone of the first Methodist chapel was laid in Bristol, May 12, 1739.

Wesley was a genius in organization. He proposed to form these societies into a United Society. His account of the formation of the United Society is as follows:

"In the latter end of the year 1739 eight or ten persons who appeared to be deeply convicted of sin, and earnestly groaning for redemption, came to Mr. Wesley in London. They desired, as did two or three more the next day, that he would spend some time with them in prayer, and advise them how to flee from the wrath to come, which they saw continually hanging over their heads. That he might have more time for this great work, he appointed a day when they all might come together; which from thenceforward they did every week, namely on Thursday, in the evening. To these, and as many more as desired to join with them (for their number increased daily), he gave advices from time to time which he judged most needful for them; and they always concluded their meetings with prayer suited to their several necessities.

"This was the rise of the United Society, first in Europe, and then in America. Such a society is no other than a company of [people] having the form and seeking the power of godliness, united in order to pray together, to receive the word of exhortation, and to watch over one another in love, that they may help each other to work out their salvation."

There was only one condition previously required of those who desired membership in the Society, viz.:

A desire to flee from the wrath to come, and be saved from their sins.

But those who desired to continue in the Society were expected to evidence their desire for salvation:

"First: by doing no harm, avoiding evil of every kind, especially that which is most generally practiced; such as, taking the name of God in vain, profaning the day of the Lord, drunkenness, buying or selling spirituous liquors, fighting, quarreling, brother going to law with brother, breaking the Golden Rule, softness, making bad debts, borrowing or buying with the probability of not paying.

"Second: by doing good of every possible sort and, as far as possible, to all [people].

"Third: by attending upon all the ordinances of God."

(See United Methodist *Discipline,* General Rules)

These simple General Rules signify the high moral standards set for early Methodists. The Methodist movement was more than a wave of religious enthusiasm. It demanded a pure motive, a joyful experience, and a blameless life.

They were not required to accept or affirm a creed. To this day conduct rather than creed is the test of membership in [The United Methodist] Church.

(Selecman, *The Methodist Primer,* pp. 16-18)

METHODISM GOES ABROAD

Methodisism spread first to Ireland and then to America. In 1766 Philip Embury, a lay preacher from Ireland, came to New York City. That same year another lay preacher from Ireland, Robert Strawbridge, came to Frederick County, Maryland. Three years later, Wesley sent Richard Boardman and Joseph Pilmore to America. In 1781, Frances Asbury came to America. He became the leader of American Methodism.

Within ten years after the first Methodist preachers arrived, American Methodism numbered about fifteen thousand members and eighty preachers. There was need for these preachers to become ordained, and Wesley requested ordination from the Bishop of London, but he refused. So Wesley himself ordained two men and appointed Dr. Thomas Coke, a presbyter in the Church of England, as a superintendent "to preside over the flock of Christ in America." Wesley directed Coke to ordain Francis Asbury as a superintendent.

On December 24, 1784, about sixty preachers gathered at the Christmas Conference in Lovely Lane Chapel in Baltimore, Maryland, and organized the Methodist Episcopal Church in America. Coke and Wesley had sent to America *The Sunday Service*, which was a briefer form of the English *Book of Common Prayer*. Twenty-four of the thirty-nine Articles of Religion of the Church of England were adopted by the Methodists. One article of religion was added, recognizing the independence of the new nation. These articles of religion are in the United Methodist *Book of Discipline*. Briefly they can be summarized as follows:

1. There is one true God, who has all power, wisdom, and goodness. He made and preserves all things. Father, Son, and Holy Spirit are one God, the Trinity.
2. Jesus, the divine Son of God, was born of the Virgin Mary, was crucified, died and was buried for the sins of men.
3. Jesus Christ rose from the dead and ascended into heaven, and will return at the last day to judge all men.
4. The Holy Spirit came from the Father and the Son and is one with them in the Trinity.
5. The Holy Scriptures (Old and New Testaments) contain all truth necessary for salvation.
6. The ancient rites and ceremonies of the Old

Testament are not binding on Christians, but its moral teachings should be obeyed.

7. Original sin is the evil in human nature which we inherit.

8. The free will of man must have divine help in order that we may do good and please God.

9. We are justified, or pardoned, not by good works, but by faith in our Lord and Savior Jesus Christ.

10. Good works are the fruits of faith and are pleasing to God.

11. It is not possible to do more good works than God requires.

12. If we sin after we are justified, or pardoned, we may repent and be forgiven.

13. The church of Christ is a congregation of faithful Christians in which the gospel is preached and the sacraments are administered.

14. Purgatory is not taught in the Bible; neither is praying to saints or worshiping images or relics.

15. Public worship should not be conducted in a language which the people do not understand. To do so is contrary to the Word of God and the custom of the early Christian church.

16. Sacraments are badges or tokens of Christian profession and signs of God's grace to us. Christ ordained only two sacraments: Baptism and the Supper of the Lord.

17. Baptism is a sign of Christian profession. The baptism of young children should be retained in the church.

18. The Sacrament of the Lord's Supper is a sign of

brotherly love and also a memorial of Christ's death. It should be observed in a spiritual manner but should not be made an object of worship.

19. In the Lord's Supper lay members should receive both bread and wine.

20. Christ's death is the only offering needed for sin. There is no value in masses for the dead. This is a dangerous deceit.

21. Ministers may marry at their own discretion.

22. It is not necessary to have the same rites and ceremonies in all places. These may be changed to meet the needs of different countries and times.

23. This article states the authority and independence of our national government.

24. Christians may possess private property, but they should give liberally to the poor.

25. A Christian may swear, when a magistrate requires it, without violating the teachings of the Bible.

DIVISIONS IN AMERICAN METHODISM

In 1828, there was an argument among Methodists over lay representation in the church. One group pulled out to become The Methodist Protestant Church.

In 1844, another division occurred. This time two issues were involved—the question of slavery and the constitutional issue over the powers of the General Conference versus the episcopacy. Both North and South kept the name Methodist Episcopal Church—the southern church merely added "South" after the name. On May 10, 1939, The Methodist Episcopal Church, The

Methodist Episcopal Church, South, and The Methodist Protestant Church united to form The Methodist Church.

In 1946, The Church of the United Brethren in Christ and The Evangelical Church united to become The Evangelical United Brethren Church. Both groups began with German-speaking Christians in the Northeast and Midwest in the early 1800s, and their first leaders had ties with the Methodists. Philip Otterbein, the founder of the United Brethren in Christ, was a friend of Francis Asbury's and took part in his ordination service. Jacob Albright, a leader in the early Evangelical Association, was a German-speaking farmer in Pennsylvania who became a Methodist preacher before beginning the Association in 1803. (See pp. 43-44.) The basic beliefs and practices of both traditions were similar to those of Methodism, and in 1968, The Methodist Church and The Evangelical United Brethren Church united to form The United Methodist Church.

The United Methodist Church embodies the history and tradition of the following churches which are Methodist in name or tradition:

The Methodist Episcopal Church

The Methodist Episcopal Church, South

The Methodist Protestant Church

The Methodist Church (merged into the Protestant Methodist Church in 1877)

United Brethren in Christ

The Evangelical Association

The United Evangelical Church

The Evangelical Church

The Methodist Church

The Evangelical United Brethren Church

1984 Statistical Review
of The United Methodist Church
Based on figures from the end of 1983*

Total lay members at the end of 1982	9,359,024
Received in 1983 on confession of faith	207,589
Received from other Methodist churches	149,624
Received from other denominations	84,746
Removed or withdrawn	193,636
Removed by transfer to other Methodist churches	125,547
Removed by transfer to other denominations	64,926
Removed by death	121,390
Total lay members	9,295,484
Total itinerant members	37,228
Total full members at end of 1983	9,332,712
Roll of military personnel	3,548
Number of organized churches	38,045
Total full connection members(ministers)	31,621
Total probationary members	3,378
Total associate members	2,229
Total conference itinerant members	37,228
Full-time local pastors under appointment	1,293
Total Annual Conference ministerial membership	38,521

*Statistics from the *1984 General Minutes of the Annual Conferences of The United Methodist Church* (Evanston, Illinois: The General Council on Finance and Administration, 1984), pp. 29, 30.

Membership in The United Methodist Church Lay and Ministerial for 1984*

Jurisdiction	Total Full Members	Total Preparatory Members	Itinerant Ministers	Under Appointment	Total Annual Conference Ministerial Membership
North Central	2,048,337	380,647	9,219	192	9,411
Northeastern	1,854,877	337,917	7,743	250	7,993
South Central	1,936,404	254,165	6,634	258	6,892
Southeastern	2,916,737	296,421	10,454	543	10,997
Western	535,581	88,230	3,178	50	3,228
Military Service	3,548	2,664			
TOTALS	9,295,484	1,360,044	37,228	1,293	38,521

*1984 General Minutes, pp. 66, 69

III

METHODISM IN AMERICA

THE METHODIST EPISCOPAL CHURCH

The first Annual Conference in American Methodism convened in St. George's Church, Philadelphia, July 14, 1773, drawing delegates from three colonies.

In the back country of Maryland, Robert Strawbridge had invited his neighbors for worship in his log house on Sam's Creek. As people were converted and more churches formed, the Baltimore Circuit was established, which reported to the Conference of 1773 thirty societies and five hundred members.

In October of 1766, Philip Embury preached to five persons in the living room of his rented house in New York. Soon the group outgrew the living room. On October 30, 1768, Embury preached the dedicatory sermon in John Street Church, believed by many to be the first Methodist church built in America.

In 1767, Captain Thomas Webb enrolled the first Methodists in Philadelphia and led them into St. George's Church. Thus Methodism in America began in the wooded hills of Frederick County, Maryland; in the small but growing port of New York; and in Philadelphia, the largest American city at that time.

Francis Asbury arrived in America from England in 1771 and immediately protested that there was insufficient "circulation of preachers." He felt that the preachers were inclined to stay in the cities rather than go out into the rural areas. By the time of the conference in 1773, Methodist preachers had driven stakes as far as Boston to the north and Norfolk and Petersburg, Virginia, to the south. However, in 1773, it is estimated there was only one Methodist among each 2,050 of America's population.

Eleven years later, the historic Christmas Conference convened in Lovely Lane Chapel, Baltimore. By 1784 America had greatly expanded to the south and west. From the Conference in 1773, ten Methodist preachers rode away from Philadelphia to their appointments, seeking to keep pace with those early American pioneers. Between 1773 and 1784 the number of circuits increased from 6 to 46; the number of preachers from 10 to 83; and the number of members from 1,160 to 14,988. Instead of one in every 2,050 persons in America being a Methodist, the ratio had decreased by 1784 to one in every 213.

The Christmas Conference gave the church a name, appointed Thomas Coke and Francis Asbury to places of administrative responsibility, and invested its ministers with an office that would command legal recognition and public respect.

Francis Asbury became the leader of American Methodism. He was a genius at planning, and he had that amazing personality which caused his associates quickly to turn to him for leadership. We Methodists today need to remember the names of some of those early preachers:

mighty evangelists like Edward Dromgoole, John Easter, and John Tunnell; scholarly preachers like William Gill, John Dickins, and William Phoebus; pathfinders like John Smith, John Major, and Jeremiah Lambert; aggressive spirits like Jesse Lee, Freeborn Garrettson, Thomas Ware, Philip Bruce, and Nelson Reed. These preachers not only penetrated frontiers and formed new churches and circuits, they were ecclesiastical architects who laid lasting foundations.

When Asbury rode to his first American preaching place, America was on horseback. When he died forty-five years later, March 31, 1816, America was on wheels. A quarter of a century later, Jason Lee preached in Oregon country. From the Atlantic coast to the Pacific coast was a long way—those wheels were wagon wheels—but Methodism made the journey. As Americans moved in every direction, Methodist preachers were there to hold revivals and start churches.

In 1786, Thomas Humphries and John Major crossed the river from South Carolina into Wilkes County, Georgia. Near the place where the first Methodist church in Georgia was started now stands Smyrna United Methodist Church, which meets in a lovely white wooden building. (I remember, as a six-year-old boy, walking down the aisle in that church and making my public profession of faith in Christ. I remember my father, J. R. Allen, who was the pastor, raising money for a monument to the first Methodist church on Georgia soil and dedicating it. That monument stands there today.) In 1788 Asbury arrived there to meet with ten preachers in the first conference ever held in Georgia.

Jesse Lee once said, "Methodism can live wherever men can live." It was proved to be so as Methodism encountered hostile Indians in Alabama and Mississippi but constantly went on farther. It is a thrilling story, how Methodism advanced through the Cumberland Gap into Kentucky and Tennessee, where settlers from North Carolina and Virginia were expanding American horizons.

After the Revolutionary War, Methodism began to enter New England, where both the physical and the cultural climates were very different from those in the Middle Atlantic and southern states. Instead of a frontier life with all its hardships and violence, New England was a land of settled and steady habits. Theology was the issue here, not evangelism. Jesse Lee, a warmhearted Virginian, led the way through the cold ecclesiastical atmosphere northward into Boston and Maine, and from the coast into regions beyond the Green Mountains of Vermont.

In the 1780s Methodism traveled west from Pennsylvania. The first Methodist sermon preached in Ohio was by George Callahan in 1787. By 1816, the year Asbury died, there were 18,150 Methodists in Ohio, a little less than one-third the entire membership of American Methodism. Methodism was also growing in Indiana and Illinois as those states increased their population. In 1804, Nathan Bangs set out from New York City for Detroit, a remote trading post. However, his preaching was not met with enthusiasm. Later, others came into that area with more success.

By 1816, the country beyond the Mississippi River was welcoming the Methodist preachers, and eight circuits were formed in Missouri along two hundred miles of the

Mississippi. It is thought that the first Methodist sermon preached in Arkansas was by William Patterson, a Kentuckian, who settled in Helena about 1800.

By the time of Asbury's death, in 1816, Methodism had increased from 10 preachers and 1,160 members in 1773 to 695 preachers and 214,235 members. That was a remarkable gain. Now Methodists numbered one in every 39 Americans. From just five communities in five eastern colonies, Methodism was now established in every state and territory east of the Mississippi except eastern Florida, which was under the control of the Spanish, and Wisconsin, which had not yet had many second-generation American settlers (most were first-generation European immigrants).

In 1845 Texas was annexed; and within two or three years, the great area from New Mexico and Colorado westward—an area which now embraces half a dozen states—became open for settlement. Soon after news spread that gold was to be found in California, the covered wagons headed west in great numbers. The Indians bitterly opposed the spread of white settlers, and much fighting was done. However, Christian people in America sent missionaries into the Wild West to evangelize the Indians with much success. In 1832 the General Conference at Philadelphia constituted a Committee on Missions, and many itinerant preachers and teachers enlisted to go to our western and northwestern frontiers. They heeded the command: "Say among the heathen that the Lord reigneth" (Psalm 96:10 KJV).

By 1833 the first settlements were being made in Iowa,

and during the next decade Methodism crossed Iowa and began building churches in Nebraska. The Plan of Separation of 1844, which divided the church into northern and southern factions, set Methodism back for a time in border areas such as Kansas, but not for long. By 1859, J. L. Dyer ("the Snowshoe Itinerant"), William H. Goode, Jerome C. Berryman, L. B. Stateler, and others, were in Colorado and organized the Denver City and Auria Mission with 22 members. Methodism was carried into the Dakotas from Iowa about 1860. In 1872 the Rocky Mountain Conference was organized, and that same year W. W. Van Orsdel ("Brother Van") began preaching across Montana. By 1865 Methodist preachers were in Utah and Wyoming.

The Oregon and California Mission Conference of The Methodist Episcopal Church was organized in 1848, and in 1853 the California Conference was organized. From these conferences Methodism came back east into Idaho, Nevada, and Arizona.

In 1890 America was linked from the Atlantic coast to the Pacific with a solid band of states, but years before this happened, the oceans were connected by Methodist conferences across our land.   •

Evangelistic passion was what built the church in America—in homes, under brush arbors, in tabernacles, in frontier churches. Wherever people could be gathered together, the gospel was preached and the invitation was given. Evangelism may not have been the only business of early Methodism, but evangelism was the main business of early Methodism.

THE UNITED BRETHREN CHURCH

In 1767, Philip Otterbein, a university graduate and minister of a German Evangelical Reformed church in Baltimore, visited a group of Mennonites in Lancaster County, Pennsylvania, and heard a Mennonite farmer, Martin Boehm, preach. After the service Otterbein greeted Martin with the words, "Wir sind Bruder" ("We are brothers"). Influenced by German pietism, Otterbein was a friend of Francis Asbury. Boehm had studied Wesley's works and eventually joined The Methodist Episcopal Church. In 1800, fourteen German ministers, including Boehm and Otterbein, met in the home of Peter Kemp, near Frederick, Maryland, beginning the practice of annual conferences; from that meeting the United Brethren Church dates its beginning. In 1815, the group formally organized, adopting a Discipline very similar to the Methodist *Book of Discipline*.

The church expanded westward in the following decades, first to Ohio, then to Indiana. Total membership grew from 10,000 in 1813, to 47,000 in 1850, and 61,000 in 1857. German immigrants increased the size of the church, but it had English-speaking members also. Thus two sets of minutes were kept at many conferences, and the *Discipline* was published in both English and German editions. In 1841, they started a missionary society, established a seminary in 1871, and formed a Women's Missionary Association in 1875. The church split in 1889 over the issue of lay delegates to general conference and some other items, but by the turn of the century there were more than 240,000 United Brethren, and by 1920 more than 340,000. In 1946 it joined with the Evangelical Alliance to form The Evangelical United Brethren Church.

THE EVANGELICAL ALLIANCE

Jacob Albright was a Lutheran farmer in Lancaster County, Pennsylvania, in the late 1700s. After the death of three of his children, he was converted through the preaching of a Methodist lay preacher. He began to study Wesley's writings and joined a Methodist class meeting. He started preaching in 1796, organizing a number of new classes. In November 1803, the leaders of the classes met and formed the Society of Evangelical Friends, with Albright as the leader. They started annual conferences in 1807, when the group reported membership of over 200. Leaders included John Walter, George Miller, Jacob Fry, and John Dreisbach. Albright was made a bishop. They also voted to create a Discipline, based on the Methodist *Discipline.*

At the first general conference in 1816, the group chose the name Evangelical Association. By 1827, there was a Western Conference for work in Ohio, and by 1837 Evangelicals had moved to the Chicago area. The General Conference of 1836 authorized the establishment of a missionary society. Later leaders included John Seybert and William Orwig. By 1900 there were 166,000 Evangelicals. The church split in 1894, primarily over the use of the German language, but also over other issues. The two groups, the United Evangelical Church and the Evangelical Association, rejoined in 1922, forming the Evangelical Church. When the Evangelical Alliance joined with the United Brethren to form The Evangelical United Brethren Church in November, 1946, the new denomination had more than 700,000 members.

IV

WHAT UNITED METHODISTS BELIEVE

Methodism from the beginning has been more life-centered than belief-centered. Yet, though Methodism has emphasized the warm heart, John Wesley was a man of scholarship who believed in education. The church he founded has emphasized from the beginning the value of a trained mind. No other church has done more to further the cause of education.

The twenty-five Articles of Religion (printed in a previous chapter of this book) are foundation beliefs of Methodist people.

The Apostles' Creed, which has come down from the early church (perhaps even as early as the second century, though its present form dates from about the seventh century), has always had a prominent place in Methodism. Today a great majority of Methodist congregations repeat this creed every Sunday.

The Apostles' Creed

I believe in God the Father Almighty, maker of heaven and earth;

And in Jesus Christ his only Son our Lord: who was conceived by Holy Spirit, born of the Virgin Mary, suffered under Pontius Pilate, was crucified, dead, and buried; the third day he rose from the dead; he ascended into heaven, and sitteth at the right hand of God the Father Almighty; from thence he shall come to judge the quick and the dead.

I believe in the Holy Spirit, the holy catholic Church, the communion of saints, the forgiveness of sins, the resurrection of the body, and the life everlasting. Amen.

The Apostles' Creed affirms seven beliefs of Christian people:
1. God the Father
2. Jesus Christ his only Son
3. The Holy Spirit
4. The church
5. Forgiveness of sins
6. The Resurrection
7. Life everlasting

Three other affirmations of faith are printed in the General Aids to Worship section of the *Book of Hymns* of The United Methodist Church. These creeds are often used in Methodist services. To carefully read the words of these creeds is inspiring.

The Nicene Creed

I believe in one God: the Father Almighty, maker of heaven and earth, and of all things visible and invisible;

And in one Lord Jesus Christ, the only begotten Son of God: begotten of the Father before all worlds, God of God, Light of Light, very God of very God, begotten, not made, being of one substance with the Father, through whom all things were made; who for us . . . and for our salvation came down from heaven, and was incarnate by the Holy Ghost of the Virgin Mary, and was made man, and was crucified also for us under Pontius Pilate; he suffered and was buried, and the third day he rose again according to the Scriptures, and ascended into heaven, and sitteth on the right hand of the Father; and he shall come again with glory, to judge both the quick and the dead; whose kingdom shall have no end.

And I believe in the Holy Ghost, the Lord, the giver of life, who proceedeth from the Father and the Son, who with the Father and the Son together is worshiped and glorified, who spake by the prophets. And I believe in the one holy catholic and apostolic Church. I acknowledge one baptism for the remission of sins. And I look for the resurrection of the dead, and the life of the world to come. Amen.

A Modern Affirmation

We believe in God the Father, infinite in wisdom, power, and love, whose mercy is over all his works, and whose will is ever directed to his children's good.

We believe in Jesus Christ, Son of God and Son of man, the gift of the Father's unfailing grace, the ground of our hope, and the promise of our deliverance from sin and death.

We believe in the Holy Spirit as the divine presence in our lives, whereby we are kept in perpetual remembrance of the truth of Christ, and find strength and help in time of need.

We believe that this faith should manifest itself in the service of love as set forth in the example of our blessed Lord, to the end that the kingdom of God may come upon the earth. Amen.

The Korean Creed

We believe in the one God, maker and ruler of all things, Father of all . . . , the source of all goodness and beauty, all truth and love.

We believe in Jesus Christ, God manifest in the flesh, our teacher, example, and Redeemer, the Savior of the world.

We believe in the Holy Spirit, God present with us for guidance, for comfort, and for strength.

We believe in the forgiveness of sins, in the life of love and prayer, and in grace equal to every need.

We believe in the Word of God contained in the Old and New Testaments as the sufficient rule both of faith and of practice.

We believe in the Church as the fellowship for worship and for service of all who are united to the living Lord.

We believe in the kingdom of God as the divine rule in human society, and in the brotherhood of man under the fatherhood of God.

We believe in the final triumph of righteousness, and in the life everlasting. Amen.

BAPTISMAL AFFIRMATION

In order to be baptized in The United Methodist Church, a youth or adult is required to affirmatively answer the following:

Do you truly and earnestly repent of your sins and accept Jesus Christ as your Savior?

Do you believe in God, the Father Almighty, maker of heaven and earth; and in Jesus Christ his only Son our Lord; and in the Holy Spirit, the Lord, the giver of life?

Do you desire to be baptized in this faith?

Will you then obediently keep God's holy will and commandments and walk in the same all the days of your life?

MEMBERSHIP VOWS

In order to become a member of The United Methodist Church, one is required to affirmatively answer the following:

Do you here, in the presence of God, and of this congregation, renew the solemn promise and vow that you made, or that was made in your name, at your Baptism?

Do you confess Jesus Christ as your Lord and Savior and pledge your allegiance to his kingdom?

Do you receive and profess the Christian faith as contained in the Scriptures of the Old and New Testaments?

Do you promise according to the grace given you to live a Christian life and always remain a faithful member of Christ's holy Church?

Will you be loyal to The United Methodist Church, and uphold it by your prayers, your presence, your gifts, and your service?

BASIC BELIEFS AND DOCTRINES OF METHODISM

It is easily seen that in order to become a member of The United Methodist Church, one does not have to subscribe to a long list of beliefs. However, the church does have a very firm and clearly stated set of beliefs. The more prominent Methodist beliefs may be briefly stated as follows:

1. *The Bible.* The Bible is the inspired and holy Word of God. The Bible is our textbook. The Bible is listed first because it is our chief source of knowledge about God and Christ and contains all the truth necessary for salvation.

2. *God.* God is infinite in wisdom, power, and love—the creator and sustainer of the universe. Every person on earth is God's child. God will hear the prayer of any and every person. One does not have to go through any intermediary to reach God. However, through worship in the sanctuary, through fellowship with other people, through proclamation of the faith from the pulpit, through study in classes, and in other ways the church helps one learn about and commune with God.

3. *Jesus Christ.* "For God so loved the world that he gave his only Son" (John 3:16). We believe Jesus Christ is uniquely God's Son, sent by God, to be born of Mary, to make the invisible God known in human form. In his expressions of loving mercy, in his teaching, in his miracles of compassion, in the absolutely holy life he lived, in the compassion of his ministry, and in the utter selflessness of his servanthood, we see God. "He who has seen me has seen the Father," Jesus said (John 14:9).

We believe Jesus Christ died upon a cross for us and our sins. His cross is an example of sacrifice, and it is a revelation of God's love, but it is more, much more. His death on the cross forever makes a difference in a person's relationship with God. As Paul put it, "God was in Christ reconciling the world to himself" (II Corinthians 5:19). We find salvation through his shed blood.

We believe Christ rose from the dead, and his resurrection is our assurance that there is life for us beyond the grave. "Because I live," he said, "You will live also" (John 14:19).

4. *The Holy Spirit.* The Holy spirit is God here on this earth—God in us and with us. The Holy Spirit came in a new and mighty way upon the Christians at Pentecost (Acts 2) and is present in the world today. We believe the Spirit bears witness to our spirits that we are in Jesus Christ and are the children of God (Romans 8:16). "The witness of the Spirit" is a doctrine often emphasized by John Wesley. In his sermon on the subject, he said, "By the witness of the Spirit I mean the inward impression on the soul, whereby the Spirit of God immediately and directly witnesses to my spirit that I am a child of God; that Jesus Christ hath loved me and given Himself for me; that all my sins are blotted out and I, even I, am reconciled to God."

5. *Forgiveness of our sins and the salvation of our souls.* This is the very center of our faith. Sin is both in our nature and in our actions. It may be said that our actions are the expressions of the sin in our souls. If we are "heartily sorry for these our misdoings," as we pray in the prayer of confession, and put our faith in Jesus Christ, we are justified, saved, cleansed—not because we deserve it, but because of the grace, the unmerited favor of God. "Therefore, since we are justified by faith, we have peace with God through our Lord Jesus Christ" (Romans 5:1).

6. *Holiness.* As the result of commitment to God we grow in faith, and our love for God and for one another becomes more complete. Holiness of heart and life has

always been emphasized by Methodists. Actually, no one ever attains a literal sinlessness in life. As one grows in Christian faith, the intentions of the soul become more perfect. This is what we call *sanctification*. "For God knew his own before ever they were, and also ordained that they should be shaped to the likeness of his Son" (Romans 8:29 NEB).

7. *Conversion.* One becomes a Christian through the Christian experience of conversion. It may be a climactic experience such as came to Saul of Tarsus as he was on the way to Damascus. Suddenly he saw a light from heaven and heard the voice of Jesus (Acts 9, 22, 24). As long as he lived, that experience was the light of his life. Throughout the history of Methodism, there have been revivals when people "came forward" to the altar in a church or revival service and received a life-changing experience in Christ. Many Methodists have been able to sing:

> I can tell you now the time,
> I can take you to the place;
> Where the Lord saved men,
> By his wonderful grace.

But there is also the experience of Timothy. He never had a climactic conversion. He could not refer to any one moment when he was converted to Christ. Writing to Timothy, Paul says, "From childhood you have been acquainted with the sacred writings which are able to instruct you for salvation through faith in Christ Jesus" (II Timothy 3:15).

John Wesley as a child was carefully instructed in the Christian faith by his wonderful mother. Throughout his life, he never forgot his early teaching. Thus it is natural that from the very beginning of the Methodist societies he would give great emphasis to teaching children. Methodism has always practiced infant baptism. It is even argued by some that Wesley organized the very first Sunday schools, preceding Robert Raikes. Methodism strongly emphasizes teaching children. No church in the world today provides finer literature for children than does The United Methodist Church, which also provides careful instruction in membership for children. Children are happily received into full membership in the church.

In the early days of Methodism, new members came out of revivals. Today the large majority of members who come on confession of faith are children. Blessed is the church which remembers the words of our Lord, "Let the children come to me, and do not hinder them; for to such belongs the kingdom of heaven" (Matthew 19:14).

Zacchaeus experienced yet a different type of conversion—a great decision. As Zacchaeus and Jesus visited together in his home, he decided to change his way of living. Jesus told him, "Today salvation has come to this house" (Luke 19:9).

Methodism has always been glad to accept the individual experience that each person has had.

8. *The Church.* The United Methodist Church recognizes and accepts all other Christian churches. We have implanted in our hearts the words of Wesley, "If your heart beats with my heart in love and loyalty to Christ, give me your hand."

All Christians are invited to the Communion table in
every United Methodist church. Methodism's invitation
to participate in the sacrament of the Lord's Supper, or
Holy Communion, is:

> Ye that do truly and earnestly repent of your sins, and are
> in love and charity with your neighbors, and intend to lead
> a new life, following the commandments of God, and
> walking from henceforth in his holy ways: Draw near with
> faith, and take this holy Sacrament to your comfort, and
> make your humble confession to almighty God. (*Book of
> Hymns,* #832)

Methodism accepts both the baptism and vows of
membership from any other Christian church. One
coming from another church is only asked, "Will you be
loyal to The United Methodist Church, and uphold it by
your prayers, your presence, your gifts, and your
service?"

Also, it has always been the custom of Methodist
churches to cooperate with other churches in every
possible way. Methodism has never claimed to be the only
church. It claims to be *one of* the Christian churches. It
has been pointed out by many that The United Methodist
Church recognizes "the Christians of other churches and
the churches of other Christians."

9. *Baptism.* Baptism is an outward sign of an inner
commitment and a spiritual new birth. It is a rite of
initiation into the body of which Christ is the head. It is
believed that three modes of baptism were practiced by
the early church: sprinkling, pouring, and immersion.
We know that these three modes continue to be practiced

by Christians today. Being more concerned about the inner experience than the outward expressions, The United Methodist Church both practices and accepts any mode of baptism. However, sprinkling is the method most often used in United Methodist churches.

FREEDOM FROM RIGID CREED

In reference to rigid creeds, Wesley made the following statement in a sermon in Glasgow:

> There is no other religious society under Heaven which requires nothing of men in order to assure their admission into it but a desire to save their souls. Look all around you; you cannot be admitted into the Church, or Society of the Presbyterian, Anabaptists, Quakers, or any other unless you hold the same opinion with them, and adhere to the same mode of worship. The Methodists alone do not insist on your holding this or that opinion; but they think and let think. Neither do they impose any particular mode of worship; but you may continue to worship in your former manner, be it what it may. Now, I do not know any other religious society, either ancient or modern, wherein such liberty of conscience is now allowed, or has been allowed, since the age of the Apostles. Here is our glorying; and a glorying peculiar to us. What Society shares it with us?

The above quotation is rather long, but it is most important in understanding The United Methodist Church today. In Wesley's day, the church in England had had enough sectarian controversies. Methodism has from the beginning been more concerned with the warm

heart and good life of the person. As one reads the
twenty-five Articles of Religion of the church (see pages
31-33) one sees they are free from dogmatic definitions or
requirements. The one thing required of those who desire
admission into The United Methodist Church has always
been a "desire to flee from the wrath to come and to be
saved from their sins." However, that desire does imply
certain convictions in the heart and mind of a person—
especially belief in God, in Jesus Christ, and in the Bible
as the sufficient rule of faith and practice. Methodism has
always believed that few doctrines are essential—we
"think and let think."

V

A SINGING CHURCH

W̲e Methodists speak often of John Wesley, but we sometimes forget Charles Wesley. After John Wesley's heart had been "strangely warmed," he first went to Charles, and it was to him he first said, "I believe." Later when they faced the question of whether or not the Methodist societies should sever their connection with the Church of England, it was Charles who said, "Church or no church, we must attend to the work of saving souls," though he was opposed to leaving the Church of England. It was Charles who so faithfully recorded the Christian experiences of those early Methodists as he wrote the hymns which they sang.

Through the years, Charles Wesley's hymns have been the binding cord of all Methodism. His hymns gave the Methodist movement life and warmth and heart. It was said of many a Methodist preacher: "He gathered a congregation about him by singing, and, after prayer, began to preach."

We can never measure the influence of hymns on Methodism. It has been said over and over that where *one* reads the sermons of John, *a thousand* sing the hymns of Charles. The first hymn in *The Book of Hymns* of our church is Charles' "O for a Thousand Tongues to Sing"—indeed, that hymn is the key note of Methodism.

O for a thousand tongues to sing,
    My great redeemer's praise,
. . . .
My gracious Master and my God,
    Assist me to proclaim . . .

There we have it—*praise* and *proclaim*. Those are the
foundation stones of an evangelistic faith. Charles Wesley
had wonderful poetic gifts which he used to do the work of
an evangelist. He wrote and he sang:

A charge to keep I have,
    A God to glorify,
A never-dying soul to save,
    And fit it for the sky.

Today it is traditional to open a Methodist Annual
Conference with Charles' stirring hymn:

And are we yet alive,
    And see each other's face?

One day Charles was standing at a window watching a
storm. The rain was pouring down from the blackened
skies. The wind was blowing hard. A dove fluttered up to
the window, cold and frightened. Charles raised the
window, took the little bird, and put it under his coat to get
it dry and warm. Gently he stroked the bird, and when the
storm had passed, he set it free. Out of that experience he
wrote:

Jesus, lover of my soul,
    Let me to thy bosom fly,
While the nearer waters roll,

While the tempest still is high:
Hide me, O my Savior, hide,
  Till the storm of life is past;
Safe into the haven guide;
  O receive my soul at last!

With lusty enthusiasm he would sing his hymn "Soldiers of Christ, arise,/And put your armor on." With deep conviction he proclaimed, "I want a principle within/Of watchful, godly fear." Joyfully he wrote and sang, "Love divine, all loves excelling."

Charles Wesley wrote six thousand hymns—maybe seven thousand, maybe more. He inspired Methodists to sing, and he still does.

As we proclaim the birth of our Lord, we sing Charles' hymn, "Hark! the herald angels sing."

As we celebrate Jesus' death, we are glad Charles wrote:

O Love divine, what has thou done!
 . . . .
  Bore all my sins upon the tree!
The Son of God for me hath died:
  My Lord, my Love, is crucified.

On Easter morning we sing with joyous enthusiasm, the hymn Charles Wesley gave us—"Christ the Lord is risen today, Alleluia!"

Victoriously we sing the hymn he wrote:

Rejoice, the Lord is King!
  Your Lord and King adore!

Many of us believe that had not Methodism been a singing church, it would never have grown and expanded as it did. Singing is a vital part of our church, and today we remember John Wesley's Directions for Singing (*Book of Hymns,* p. vii):

   I.   Learn these tunes before you learn any others; afterwards learn as many as you please.

  II.   Sing them exactly as they are printed here, without altering or mending them at all; and if you have learned to sing them otherwise, unlearn it as soon as you can.

 III.   Sing all. See that you join with the congregation as frequently as you can. Let not a slight degree of weakness or weariness hinder you. If it is a cross to you, take it up, and you will find it a blessing.

  IV.   Sing lustily and with a good courage. Beware of singing as if you were half dead, or half asleep; but lift up your voice with strength. Be no more afraid of your voice now, nor more ashamed of its being heard, than when you sung the songs of Satan.

   V.   Sing modestly. Do not bawl, so as to be heard above or distinct from the rest of the congregation, that you may not destroy the harmony; but strive to unite your voices together, so as to make one clear melodious sound.

  VI.   Sing in time. Whatever time is sung be sure to keep with it. Do not run before nor stay behind it; but attend close to the leading voices, and move therewith as exactly as you can; and take care not to sing too slow. This drawling way naturally steals on all who are lazy; and it is high time to drive it out from us, and sing all our tunes just as quick as we did at first.

VII. Above all sing spiritually. Have an eye to God in every word you sing. Aim at pleasing him more than yourself, or any other creature. In order to do this attend strictly to the sense of what you sing, and see that your heart is not carried away with the sound, but offered to God continually; so shall your singing be such as the Lord will approve here, and reward you when he cometh in the clouds of heaven.

VI

THE UNITED METHODIST CHURCH AND SOCIAL CONCERNS

When Methodism left the British Isles to cross the Atlantic, it left something it has been a long time in recovering—the deep social concerns of its founder. John Wesley believed both in the experience of faith and its practice—an emotional experience—a program of action. In his mind, the four greatest evils of his day were poverty, war, ignorance, and disease. For more than half a century he waged war on these enemies of society, and in his struggles the social conscience of today was born.

There are sufficient reasons why American Methodism did not carry the banner of Wesley's war against the enemies of society. Those social problems were not found in early America, which in the late 1700s was a rural frontier society. It was a land of boundless opportunity, and for the most part a homogeneous society. The great need in America was evangelism, and those early Methodist circuit riders developed an evangelism unparalleled in the world, before or since. Revival fires were lighted, souls were saved, churches were established.

Now the situation in America has vastly changed. In our society today there are poor and hungry people. In our population in the United States, there are people from every race and society of this earth, and prejudices need to be confronted. Today we face the threat of nuclear war with its power of destruction far greater than anything Wesley could even imagine. Great progress has been made in the war against ignorance and disease, but there is still a long way to go.

Today, American Methodism is in the act of rediscovering our church's founder. If this chapter seems to be more labored than the others in this small volume, it is because the need just now in our society is so great. On social issues, let us be re-introduced to our church father.

WEALTH

What did Wesley say about *wealth*? We read again his sermon "The Use of Money," which sums up his view. We are to gain wealth only in ways that do not injure ourselves in mind or body, because to gain wealth in this way would be "buying gold too dear." Neither must our accumulation injure any other person.

However, wealth does not belong to the one who accumulates it. Only God owns; people are the stewards. We are to render unto God everything—"not a tenth, not a third, not half, but all that is God's." Caring for one's family is a part of God's work. Next, if "there be an overplus left," then "do good to them that are of the household of faith"; and "if there be an overplus still, 'do good unto all men.' "

Wesley had a severe doctrine of stewardship, and he felt that those who did not live by it "were not only robbing God, continually embezzling and wasting their Lord's goods, but also robbing the poor, the hungry, the naked; wronging the widow and the fatherless; and making themselves accountable for all the want, affliction, and distress which they may, but do not, remove." Strong words!

Wesley was so dedicated to his stewardship convictions that he could write: "If I leave behind me ten pounds . . . you and all mankind bear witness against me that I lived and died a thief and a robber." He practiced his philosophy and died practically in poverty. He believed that the poor had certain rights and that, when half the people were burdened by wealth and half by poverty, human rights had been robbed.

Wesley went far beyond the old "charity" attitude. More than any other person he was the founder of modern philanthropy. *Charity* relieves only the immediate pain. *Philanthropy* seeks to cure the diseases of society. Philanthropy recognizes one's debt to society. The broken pipes in society must be repaired so that the water of life can flow to all people.

The first stage in giving is *charity*, the second stage is *philanthropy*, but Wesley also referred to the third stage, *social justice*, which recognizes that all people have rights to the good things of God's earth without being made objects of either charity or philanthropy. Since the days of Wesley, the church has had a growing insight into the meaning of a Christian social order—one which gives both the weak and the less fortunate a proper opportunity.

In Wesley's day poverty was accepted either as God's will for the poor, or as a demonstration of the fact that there was not enough wealth for everybody, or that the poor were lazy and did not want to work. In reference to poverty, Wesley said: "What remedy is there for this sore evil? Many thousand poor people are starving. Find them work, and you will find them meat. They will earn and eat their own bread. But how can the masters [employers] give them work without ruining themselves? Procure vent [sale] for what is wrought [made] and the masters [employers] give them as much work as they can do. And this would be done by sinking the price of provisions; for then people would have money to buy other things."

Some would condemn Wesley for seeming to advocate a controlled economy. It was not economic theories but human hurt which motivated him. He saw a woman "picking up from a dunghill stinking sprouts, and carrying them home for herself and her children." He saw another "gathering the bones which dogs had left in the streets." To him poverty was a national shame "in a land flowing, as it were, with milk and honey! abounding with all the necessities, the conveniences, the superfluities of life!" The nation must respond.

Our Social Creed

We believe in God, Creator of the world; and in Jesus Christ the Redeemer of creation. We believe in the Holy Spirit, through whom we acknowledge God's gifts, and we repent of our sin in misusing these gifts to idolatrous ends.

We affirm the natural world as God's handiwork and dedicate ourselves to its preservation, enhancement, and faithful use by humankind.

We joyfully receive, for ourselves and others, the blessings of community, sexuality, marriage, and the family.

We commit ourselves to the rights of men, women, children, youth, young adults, the aging, and those with handicapping conditions; to improvement of the quality of life; and to the rights and dignity of racial, ethnic, and religious minorities.

We believe in the right and duty of persons to work for the good of themselves and others, and in the protection of their welfare in so doing; in the rights to property as a trust from God, collective bargaining, and responsible consumption; and in the elimination of economic and social distress.

We dedicate ourselves to peace throughout the world, to freedom for all peoples, and to the rule of justice and law among nations.

We believe in the present and final triumph of God's Word in human affairs, and gladly accept our commission to manifest the life of the gospel in the world. Amen.

(*Book of Discipline,* p. 104)

EDUCATION

Wesley was a constant and determined enemy of ignorance. Long before his experience of the warm heart, he knew the meaning of the trained mind. The first eleven years of his life were spent in the school his mother established in their home for her many children. She believed she could improve on the methods used in her day in instructing and governing children, and she proved it. Each child was expected to master the alphabet by the age of five.

Not only did Susanna Wesley teach her children the educational subjects, she also set apart an hour a week when she would meet with each child alone for prayer and religious instruction. Thus John Wesley grew up relating religion and education, and for him there was never any conflict between the two. In his heart and ministry, religion and education were married and they always remained as one, each supporting the other.

For five years Wesley was a student in Charterhouse School, London. Then he attended Oxford University, where he received the degree of master of arts—equivalent to our Ph.D. today.

At Oxford he developed his daily plan of study, which was: Mondays and Tuesdays, Greek and Latin; Wednesdays, logic and ethics; Thursdays, Hebrew and Arabic; Fridays, metaphysics and natural philosophy; Saturdays, oratory and poetry; Sundays, divinity.

He never stopped studying. During his ministry he published 440 books, tracts, and pamphlets. One of his most famous phrases he wrote while a student at Oxford: "Leisure and I have taken leave of each other"—and so it was all his life.

The undying contribution Wesley made to education was not in the realm of theory or techniques. The world has moved far beyond him in these areas. What gives Wesley an everlasting place in the history of education was his conviction that all are equal before God and therefore the poor are as much entitled to the blessings of an education as are the rich or the high-born. Green the historian said that Wesley "gave the first impulse to our popular education."

Wesley promoted planned studies for his preachers, literature for the masses of people, the Kingswood School for the sons of his preachers (today he would have included the daughters), and the development of the

Sunday school. He established a school for the poor at the Foundry, in London, and one for orphans in Newcastle.

However, as Methodism moved to America, educational concerns were not nearly so strong. In fact, professional education for the ministry was suspect in American Methodism for a long time. Cokesbury College was established early, but when it was destroyed by fire in 1795, after eight years of not too successful operation, many Methodists thought it might be a sign that Methodists should not build colleges.

The first Methodist theological school was established in Newbury, Vermont, in 1841. It was moved to Concord, New Hampshire, in 1847 and was named Methodist General Bible Institute. In 1867 it was moved to Boston and in 1871 became the Boston University School of Theology. In 1854 Garrett Biblical Institute was founded in Evanston, Illinois, and Drew Theological Seminary in 1867 in New Jersey.

Later the Methodist attitude toward education began to change, and the church began to found colleges—Randolph-Macon Woman's College, Lynchburg, Virginia, 1830; Wesleyan University, Middletown, Connecticut, 1831; Allegheny College, Meadville, Pennsylvania, 1817, which became associated with Methodist interests in 1833; Dickinson College, Carlisle, Pennsylvania, 1783, which became associated with Methodism in 1834. Expansion to the west and south was rapid; and by the time of the Civil War, Methodism had established thirty-four colleges which remain today.

The Evangelical Association founded Union Seminary in 1854, in New Berlin, Pennsylvania, which became

Albright College, and later Central Pennsylvania College in Reading. Plainfield College was founded in 1862 in Plainfield, Illinois, and in 1870 moved to Naperville, changing its name to North Central College in 1926. Other schools were founded in the Midwest and West, but only three of those founded before 1890 became permanent institutions.

The United Brethren founded Otterbein College in 1847 in Westerville, Ohio, and Lebanon Valley College, Annville, Pennsylvania in 1866. Other schools were founded in the Midwest, some of which were merged or grew slowly.

In addition to colleges, there was a great need in America for high schools. Many Methodist academies were established and remained strong until public education met the need in their communities.

Today The United Methodist Church has 104 colleges in 38 states and the District of Columbia. There are nine secondary schools and one elementary school. It has 13 seminaries, schools of theology, or graduate schools.

SUNDAY SCHOOLS

In speaking of education, let us not overlook the Sunday schools. In 1983, in United Methodist churches, there were 138,730 Sunday schools with 4,068,179 enrolled. This constitutes both teaching and evangelistic opportunities. Many of us Methodists were carried to Sunday school as babies. We grew up feeling that we belonged. Before we ever learned to read, we were taught basic principles of the Christian faith; and many of us grew up believing ourselves to be Christians and never knowing ourselves to be anything else.

The educational process goes on throughout one's life. In The United Methodist Church, the church school is concerned about every age, not only children. Methodism has a very effective program for youth. An important emphasis today is on "singles," especially in metropolitan areas, where there are very large numbers of single young adults. This group is an important part of any church program. Couples' classes, for both younger and older couples, are given much attention. There are inter-generational groupings. And in United Methodist church schools, loving attention is given to senior citizens' groups. The educational process covers the entire lifespan and The United Methodist Church never gives up on the impossible task—the perfection of human character.

THE UNITED METHODIST PUBLISHING HOUSE

Supporting and undergirding the educational program of our churches is The United Methodist Publishing House.

According to legend, Martin Luther once threw his ink bottle at the devil. But John Wesley hurled an entire printing press at him! Francis Asbury wisely said that the religious press "is next in importance to the preaching of the gospel."

Four weeks after George Washington became President of the United States (March 4, 1789) twenty-five Methodist preachers met in John Street Chapel, New York City, and founded The Methodist Publishing House.

However, the tradition of Methodist publishing goes back to John Wesley himself, who was constantly involved in the book business. He taught both preachers and lay people to read books and trained his preachers to sell books. He spent many hours editing classics for lay people, translating books from Latin, Greek, and German, so that Methodists could read the best that Christians had written through the ages. United Methodists should never forget that their founder was the most prolific author and publisher of his time. He earned and gave away $150,000 through publishing (equivalent to several million dollars today).

In America, John Dickins was the first book steward. The progress of this enterprise is indicated by the following quotation from *The Story of The Methodist Publishing House*: "At the time of unification [in 1939], the publishing interests of the Church consisted of two corporations of The Methodist Episcopal Church with houses in New York, Cincinnati, Chicago, Boston, Pittsburgh, Detroit, Kansas City, San Francisco, and Portland, Oregon: one corporation of the Methodist Episcopal Church, South, with houses in Nashville, Dallas and Richmond; and one corporation of the Methodist Protestant Church, with houses in Baltimore and Pittsburgh. The corporations were preserved under the new Board of Publication." Today there is one central headquarters of The United Methodist Publishing House, in Nashville, Tennessee, with 48 retail Cokesbury bookstores and three service centers coast to coast. More than two million books were printed and bound in 1984. Approximately fifteen million copies of curriculum resources go out from the Publishing House every year, including 400,000 records, 250,000 feet of film and more than 10,000 cassettes. In addition about 93 million church bulletins and inserts are printed and distributed. The printing plant in Nashville is the largest denominationally owned printing and book-manufacturing plant in the world. It provides printing services for other groups, and its total output is 150 million items each year in addition to curriculum pieces.

From the beginning, the proceeds of the Publishing House have been used to help support retired Methodist ministers and their dependents. In 1984, the total appropriation to conference claimants was $1,000,000. This brought the total distributed since the founding of the Publishing House to $43,413,573.

This is a magnificent record of conscientious and successful management.

Each week vast numbers of pieces of literature are circulated in classes and groups within local church schools. This literature deals with lessons from the Bible, doctrines of the church, and problems that confront children, youth, adults, and the home. Able writers discuss social conditions and all manner of questions that arise in our complex civilization. No church surpasses ours in its literature, and few churches have reached our high standard of excellence and adaptability to the need of these millions of people in country, village, and city. This great volume of wholesome reading matter is as good seed scattered abroad. Its influence in forming high ideals and molding Christian character cannot be overstated.

The *Book of Discipline of The United Methodist Church*

provides for the organization of the children's division, the youth division, and the adult division in each church school. The purpose is stated as follows:

"To explore the meanings of the Christian faith in all its dimensions, to discover and appropriate to persons those meanings which are relevant for their lives and for society, and to assume personal responsibility for expressing those meanings in all their relationships. Through such experiences, persons will be encouraged to commit themselves to Christ and to unite with the Christian community through membership in a local church. The Board of Discipleship sets standards and provides guidance resources and plans for the organization, administration, grouping, and leadership of the church school."

All the concerns of the church are present in the church school's educational ministry: Christian unity and interreligious concerns, church and society, evangelism, higher education, stewardship, worship, missions, and religion and race.

President Eisenhower once said, "I see no hope for the world except education, but I am most optimistic for the world because I believe in education." The United Methodist Church believes in education.

WESLEY AND WAR

Wesley was passionate in the denunciation of war. His conviction was that if people cannot settle their differences by reason and calm judgment, then certainly nothing would be settled by war. Wesley said:

Whatever be the cause, let us calmly and impartially consider the thing itself. Here are forty thousand men gathered together on this plain. What are they going to do? See, there are thirty or forty thousand more at a little distance. And these are going to shoot them through the head or body, to stab them or split their skulls, and send most of their souls into everlasting fire, as fast as they possibly can. Why so? What harm have they done to them? O none at all! They do not so much as know them. But, a man who is King of France, has a quarrel with another man, who is King of England. So these Frenchmen are to kill as many of these Englishmen as they can to prove the King of France is in the right. Now, what an argument is this! What a method of proof! What an amazing way of deciding controversies!

In Wesley's mind, war was totally against all reason and common sense. One can only wonder what he would say in reference to the destructive power of war today.

Methodism has always held high Wesley's banner— "The world is my parish." That means a loving concern for the welfare of each and every person on earth. War is the antithesis of universal love. Though Methodism has never embraced pacifism, though United Methodist churches proudly fly the flag of their country, though United Methodist people have gone forth in defense of their country—still Methodism stands firm in its support for peace on earth and good will toward all people.

Sherwood Eddy summed up the First World War in the words: "The saddest thing is not that some ten million of our people are dead, that the world is impoverished, victimized, embittered by hate, rent by suspicion and fear. The saddest thing is that we settled nothing, made nothing safe, achieved no lasting good."

One of the strongest satires against war is that which Mark Twain wrote in the form of a prayer:

O Lord our God, help us to tear their soldiers to bloody shreds with our shells;

Help us to cover their smiling fields with the pale forms of their patriot dead;

Help us to drown the thunder of the guns with the wounded, writhing in pain;

Help us to lay waste their humble homes with a hurricane of fire;

Help us to wring the hearts of their unoffending widows with unavailing grief;

Help us to turn them out rootless with their little children to wander unfriended through wastes of their desolate land;

For ourselves, who adore thee, Lord, blast their hopes, blight their lives, protract their bitter pilgrimage, make heavy their steps, water their way with their tears, stain the white snow with the blood of their wounded feet!

We ask of one who is the Spirit of Love and who is the ever faithful refuge and friend of those who are sorely beset, and seek his aid with humble and contrite hearts.

Grant our prayer, O Lord, and thine shall be the praise and honor and glory now and ever. Amen.

The reading of the above words strengthens us in our mission to join hands with people of good will over all the earth and seek the elimination of all war.

Basil Mathews, walking in the dusty streets of an Arabian village, met a tall young Arab boy playing a flute. He asked to see the flute, for it seemed a heavy, awkward thing; on examining it, he found that it was made out of an old gun barrel. The boy explained that he had picked up an old gun on a near-by battlefield, filed it down, drilled holes in it, and out of a weapon of destruction had created an instrument of music.

"Swords into plowshares . . . spears into pruning hooks," wrote the prophet Micah (4:3). We can add, Weapons of destruction into instruments of music. Our church is dedicated to peace among all people.

HUMAN SUFFERING

As one reads even a few pages of Wesley's *Journal*, it is clearly seen that the founder of Methodism was first concerned with the saving of souls, and his next consuming desire was to relieve people's physical distress and see them well in body. Early in his ministry he had groups of volunteers carefully organized and regularly visiting the sick in London. He divided London into twenty-three sections and assigned two visitors to each section. Not only were they to bring comfort to the sick, these visitors were trained both to inquire into the spiritual state of the people and to discover their physical needs. The visitors were to seek medical advice and try to provide for the physical needs of the people. Weekly the visitors were to report to the societies.

Wesley made arrangements for medicine for the poor and set aside Fridays for receiving the sick poor at his house in London. It was not long before "medicines were occasionally given to about five hundred persons." This service was not limited to members of the Society but was available for whoever needed it. Each Methodist society became an agency to serve the sick, the poor, and the needy.

Wesley's concern for the poor is seen in his writings. He published "A Collection of Recipes for the Use of the Poor." This was a compilation of simple remedies for the more common ailments. In 1747, he wrote and published "Primitive Physic: or an Easy and Natural Method of Curing Most Diseases."

It is no surprise that out of the church which Wesley established has come a great stream of serving institutions—hospitals, homes and facilities for children, young people, the handicapped, and the aging, all of which are under the Health and Welfare Ministries Department of the Board of Global Ministries. It is inspiring to realize that there are 72 hospitals in 26 states serving both the cause of medicine and The United Methodist Church.

Sixty-four United Methodist-related facilities in 31 states offer child care to their communities. Many of these are homes for children with one or both parents missing. Some also offer help for unwed mothers. There are 214 retirement communities, homes, or nursing homes for the elderly run by Methodists in 40 states plus the District of Columbia. Twenty-six states offer some form of health-care facilities other than hospitals. In addition, five states have ministries to the handicapped.

UNITED METHODISM AND RACIAL CONCERNS

The Pilgrims from England landed on American shores in 1620. They came to this country seeking religious freedom. The cultures and ideals of the Pilgrims became a strong force in developing our American way of life. They came by choice, fleeing from very unhappy religious persecution. Every year during the Thanksgiving season, we especially remember the Pilgrim settlers with joy and appreciation.

However, blacks preceded the Pilgrims by six months. They came to America by force, not by choice. Happy in their native land of Africa, they were captured by slave traders and brought to our shores. They were reduced from proud, independent people to mere slaves. This is one of the most shameful stories in the long history of humanity.

The record of the traditionally white churches in reference to black people has not been all that it should have been. The United Methodist Church takes some pride in the fact that it has been as active as any other church in America on behalf of the rights of black people. In no other church in America today do black people have a stronger place and give greater leadership.

In Harriet Beecher Stowe's novel *Uncle Tom's Cabin*, Uncle Tom says to his master, "You own my body, but not my soul." This statement expresses the strength of these people through centuries. In spite of conditions, they kept their religious faith. The thrilling story of black people in America is that they have kept climbing upward.

Black people have been an important part of American Methodism from the beginning. The first black to become a local preacher was Black Harry Hoosier, who was a servant to Francis Asbury. Though Harry was unable to read or write, he was a born orator, and some have suggested that he was the most popular preacher in the church of his time.

In the early years the black membership in the church grew rapidly, and in 1844, there were 145,000 black members in the Methodist Church. However, with the division in 1844, the church lost most of its black members. Two years later, in 1846, there were only 30,000 blacks. Those who were in the Methodist Episcopal Church, South, after emancipation, were organized in 1870 into a separate denomination known as the Colored Methodist Episcopal Church, which still exists today as the Christian Methodist Episcopal Church.

When three branches of Methodism became The Methodist Church in 1939, the church was divided into six regions (jurisdictions), with blacks having the Central Jurisdiction. At the time, this was considered the best practical solution. In 1968 the Central Jurisdiction was merged into the other five jurisdictions, and today black people have taken their rightful place in the church as a whole.

Increasingly through the years, black people have wanted discriminatory impediments removed and opportunities given on the basis of merit. Large numbers of black Methodists wanted to be recognized as an important part of the church community, accepting both the privileges and responsibilities of members of the church. Happily this is now an accomplished reality within the structural organization of The United Methodist Church. Today black people are giving strong leadership within the church and making distinct contributions.

————

Wesley's life, his preaching, and his entire ministry became a proclamation of social Christianity. He said: "Solitary religion is not to be found [in the Gospel of Christ]. 'Holy Solitaires' is a phrase no more consistent with the Gospel than holy adulterers. The Gospel of Christ knows no religion but social; no holiness but social holiness. . . . This we have from Christ that he who loves God, loves his brother also. . . . He feels in his soul a burning restless desire of spending and being spent for them."

Let it be emphasized that today United Methodism has a social mission. The term *social gospel* unfortunately implies to some people that there are two gospels—one social and the other individual. Let us reaffirm the fact that there is only one gospel. Christianity is a social religion in the sense that when an individual experiences Christ, that individual has a changed attitude toward society. Until the world and society in which we live can be called the kingdom of God, then Methodism will have a social mission.

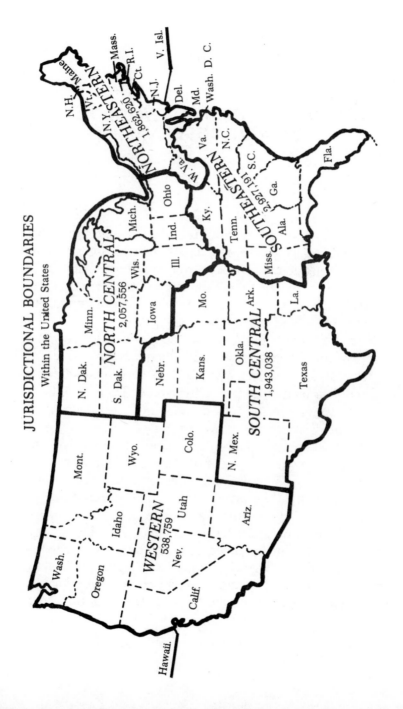

JURISDICTIONAL BOUNDARIES
Within the United States

NORTHEASTERN
1,862,620

SOUTHEASTERN
2,927,191

NORTH CENTRAL
2,057,556

SOUTH CENTRAL
1,943,038

WESTERN
538,759

VII

THE UNITED METHODIST CHURCH GOVERNMENT

From the beginning, The United Methodist Church and its forerunners have been well organized. At the organization in 1784 all powers resided in that body of preachers. They had the authority to enact or repeal any legislation. At first it was planned to have a conference of all the preachers once a year. Bishop Asbury adopted the custom of holding the yearly conference by sections across the church. That plan did not turn out to be practical, so an effort was made to govern the church through a council of presiding elders. Then in 1792 a General Conference was called, and the quadrennial General Conference was created. It was to be a conference including all the preachers. However, due to the rapid growth of the church and the distances to be traveled, the General Conference of 1808 created our present plan of government by a delegated General Conference. This meant that conferences remote from the site of the General Conference would be equally represented. The first delegated conference was in 1812.

In 1870 the College of Bishops was assigned judicial as well as executive functions. They gave to the College of Bishops powers not unlike those of the U.S. Supreme

Court. In 1934 the General Conference officially set up the Judicial Council, which became a part of The Methodist Church. The Judicial Council is composed of five ministers and four lay persons, and "all appellate power" is vested in this council. All decisions of the Judicial Council are final. This is Methodism's Supreme Court.

In The United Methodist Church there are now six conferences. To each conference there are certain duties or functions assigned by the General Conference. The conferences are as follows:

1. The General Conference, which meets once in four years.
2. The Jurisdictional Conference, which meets once in four years.
3. The Annual Conference, which meets once a year.
4. The District Conference
5. The Charge Conference
6. The Church Conference

THE GENERAL CONFERENCE

The General Conference is the one lawmaking body of The United Methodist Church. It alone can speak for the church. It determines the conditions, privileges, and duties of church membership; the powers and duties of the other conferences of the church; and the nature, function, and qualifications of the ordained ministry and the diaconal ministry. The General Conference is authorized to initiate and direct all connectional enterprises of the church, and to provide boards for their promotion and administration.

The General Conference meets every four years and is composed equally of lay and ministerial members (about nine hundred), who have been elected by the Annual Conferences. The General Conference is subject to the Restrictive Rules, which are part of the Constitution of the church. They provide that:

1. The General Conference shall not revoke or change our Articles of Religion.
2. It shall not "do away with the episcopacy or destroy the plan of our itinerant general superintendency."
3. Ministers and members may not be expelled from the church without a trial.
4. The General Conference shall not revoke or change the General Rules.
5. The produce of the Publishing House is secured to the benefit of "retired or disabled preachers, their spouses, widows, or widowers, and children."

THE JURISDICTIONAL CONFERENCE

The United Methodist Church has five Jurisdictional Conferences: Northeastern, Southeastern, North Central, South Central, and Western. The Annual Conferences in each jurisdiction elect the delegates to the Jurisdictional Conference; delegates are comprised equally of ministers and lay persons. The primary functions of each Jurisdictional Conference are to elect bishops, to determine the boundaries of episcopal areas, to assign bishops, and to implement General Conference legislation.

THE ANNUAL CONFERENCE

As the name indicates, the Annual Conference of each designated area meets once a year. Not only is this conference composed of ministerial members, but every church or charge is represented by delegates who are laypersons. This is the basic body in the church. It votes on all constitutional amendments; elects delegates to General and Jurisdictional conferences; has responsibility for all matters relating to ministerial character and orders; hears reports of councils, committees, boards, and agencies; and lays plans for the work of the coming year. The bishop in charge presides over the Annual Conference. The pastoral appointments are made at this conference, though pastors may be assigned at other times.

THE DISTRICT CONFERENCE

A District Conference shall be held if directed by the Annual Conference of which it is a part, and may be held upon the call of the district superintendent. A District Conference shall be composed of members determined and specified by the Annual Conference. This conference may administer district real and personal property, form a district lay program, and organize a district Council on Ministries. There is a district Committee on Ordained Ministry, a Committee on District Superintendency, and a district organization named United Methodist Women.

THE CHARGE CONFERENCE

The Charge Conference is made up of members of the Administrative Board (or Boards, if more than one church is on the pastoral charge). The district superintendent, or a minister whom he or she designates, presides at the meetings. This conference meets annually and at other times when it is called. It has general supervision of the work of the local church.

THE CHURCH CONFERENCE

This conference is open to all members of the church and may consider any matter pertaining to the local church. Regulations governing the call and conduct of the Charge Conference also apply to the Church Conference.

TRUSTEES AND CHURCH PROPERTY

Each local church or charge must have a Board of Trustees, which holds the property of the church in trust and must act according to the will of the Charge or Church Conference. The trust clause in deeds to church and parsonage property provides that the property is under the direction of The United Methodist Church.

GENERAL COUNCIL OF MINISTRIES

The General Council on Ministries is for the purpose of facilitating the fulfillment of the objectives of mission and program-related policies of the General Conference. Membership on the council consists of one member from each Annual Conference and Missionary Conference within the United States and Puerto Rico. The following agencies are accountable to the General Council on Ministries: the general boards of Church and Society, Discipleship, Global Ministries, Higher Education and Ministry, and the general commissions on Christian Unity and Interreligious Concerns, Religion and Race, and the Status and Role of Women.

GENERAL COUNCIL ON FINANCE AND ADMINISTRATION

The General Council on Finance and Administration is amenable to the General Conference. It receives and disburses all general church funds and works with all the general agencies in matters pertaining to budgets and fiscal responsibilities.

COUNCIL OF BISHOPS

The United Methodist Church is "episcopal" in its form of government. The bishops are the chief executives and administrative leaders of the church. They serve for life and assume "residential and presidential" duties until their retirement on or before their seventieth birthday. In addition to presiding over local conferences, they give churchwide and ecumenical leadership. Throughout the history of the church our bishops have both deserved and received honor and respect, and we look to our bishops for leadership.

CENTRAL CONFERENCES

Central Conferences are those conferences of The United Methodist Church outside the United States.

They have their own bishops and administrative officers, determine the boundaries of the Annual Conferences within their respective areas, and implement the legislation of the General Conference.

THE COUNCIL ON MINISTRIES
IN THE LOCAL CHURCH

The Council on Ministries of each local church is to consider, develop, and coordinate goals and program proposals for the church's mission. The Council is concerned with the entire program of the local church, including children's ministries, youth ministries, adult ministries, family ministries, education, evangelism, health and welfare, stewardship, higher education and campus ministries, church and society, Christian unity and interreligious concerns, religion and race, communications, missions, and worship.

The local Council on Ministries reports to the Administrative Board.

UNITED METHODIST WOMEN

United Methodist Women is a part of the local church, and membership is open to any woman who indicates her desire to belong and to participate in the global mission of the church. Throughout many, many years, the organized women in the church have made important contributions.

Many churches also have an organization of United Methodist Men.

THE PASTOR

In The United Methodist Church ordained ministers are appointed by the bishop to local churches and other fields of labor. The pastor's duties are, among others, to preach the Word, administer the sacraments, give pastoral care and leadership, instruct candidates for membership, perform the marriage ceremony, counsel bereaved families and conduct appropriate memorial services for the dead, visit and counsel members and families, and give general leadership and oversight to the local church.

Ministerial members of the conference may be appointed by the bishop to serve in ministries beyond the local church.

THE DIACONAL MINISTER

Diaconal ministers are people called and set apart for representative ministries of leadership within the body of the church, to help the whole of the membership of the church be engaged in and fulfill its ministry of service. Many directors of Christian education, directors of music, and business administrators within the church are diaconal ministers.

Diaconal ministers are related to the general church through the Conference Board of Diaconal Ministry, their work reviewed annually by it and the cabinet, and approved by the bishop of the Annual Conference. They are directly responsible to the local church or agency in which they serve. Their relationship to an Annual Conference of The

United Methodist Church is conferred by the act of
consecration performed by the bishop of the conference.

COMMITTEE ON PASTOR-PARISH RELATIONS

The Committee on Pastor-Parish Relations, composed
of not fewer than five and not more than nine laypersons,
is elected by the Charge Conference. This committee
counsels with the pastor and other staff members; makes
recommendations to the Administrative Board as to
persons to be employed; and consults on matters
pertaining to pulpit supply, proposals for salaries and
other compensations; and cooperates with the pastor(s),
the district superintendent, and the bishop in securing
clergy leadership. Its relationship to the district superintendent and the bishop is advisory only.

THE DISTRICT SUPERINTENDENT

The district superintendent is appointed by the bishop
from among the ministers of the Annual Conference to
supervise the work of a given district. Districts may vary in
size from about twenty pastoral charges in sparsely settled
areas to sixty or more in metropolitan areas. The district
superintendent is appointed each year but may be
reassigned for a maximum of six successive years. The
district superintendent travels and preaches throughout
the district, supervises the affairs of the churches in the
district, represents the pastors and churches of the district
in the bishop's cabinet, and helps plan and support the
work of the entire conference. The district superintendent
is a very important person in the polity of Methodism.

VIII

UNITED METHODISM'S WORLD MISSION

The development of the missionary zeal in Methodism may be summarized in three of Wesley's own statements: "About a quarter before nine . . . I felt my heart strangely warmed"; "I am a Priest of the Church Universal"; and "The world is my parish."

Our United Methodist Church in America came into being because of the missionary spirit, and our church has never lost its mission vision. No obstacle has been able to halt the Methodist missionaries. "Go therefore and make disciples of all nations, baptizing them in the name of the Father and of the Son and of the Holy Spirit, teaching them to observe all that I have commanded you; and lo, I am with you always, to the close of the age" (Matthew 28:19). This is a command of Jesus Christ which The United Methodist Church takes literally. All the following countries experience some measure of United Methodist ministry:

Algeria	Austria	Brazil
Angola	Belgium	Bulgaria
Argentina	Bolivia	Burma

Canada
Central Congo
Chile
Costa Rica
Cuba
Czechoslovakia
Denmark
Dominican
  Republic
Ecuador
Finland
France
Germany
Hong Kong
Hungary
India

Indonesia
Japan
Korea
Liberia
Malaya
Mexico
Mozambique
Nepal
Nigeria
Norway
Okinawa
Pakistan
Panama
Peru
Philippines
Poland

Puerto Rico
Rhodesia
Sarawak
Sierra Leone
Singapore
South Africa
Southern Congo
Sweden
Switzerland
Taiwan
United States
  of America
Uruguay
Yugoslavia
Zambia

A PERSONAL EXPRESSION

I love The United Methodist Church because:
The church sent her itinerant ministers into the mountain areas of the Southeast and won my ancestors to a life of piety and service as disciples of Jesus Christ.

The church sought my father in those distant hills, put something into his heart, claimed his life, and gave him a place of service as a Methodist preacher. The night he died, he said to me, "It's all right. I have the faith."

The church brought a young girl into the fellowship, gave to her the highest ideals, a beautiful and dedicated Christian spirit. She was my mother.

The church quickly claimed me for the kingdom of God and gave me opportunities to go to school and fulfill my mission in life as a preacher.

The church brought me into fellowship with Christian people and into fellowship with God. The church led me to believe in Jesus Christ and to accept him as my Savior and Lord.

The church blessed my marriage and helped my wife and me to claim our children for Christ.

The United Methodist Church is the best thing that ever happened to me.

I love my church.

Charles L. Allen